Unpacking the Emotional Suitcase

An Activity Guide for Emotional Success

Tierica Berry

Unpacking the Emotional Suitcase

Published by:
Affirmative Expression
PO Box 360856
Decatur, GA 30036

Cover design by:

Chozy R. Aiyub
Info@chozydesigns.com
www.Chozydesigns.com

Printed in the United States of America

ISBN: 978-0-9963605-1-7

Dedication

I know some people that have been let down so many times that it is hard to trust anyone ever again. I know people that have been neglected and abandoned making it hard to form new relationships. I have met individuals that have been abused physically, mentally, and emotionally and have decided to never give anyone that much power over their life again. Then there are those that have never been told they were smart, beautiful, or valuable so they allow people to treat them like they are dumb, ugly, or worthless. There are so many broken people in our communities and even in our families. No more will we turn a blind eye to these bleeding hearts. I dedicate this book to everyone who is ready to take action and begin Unpacking The Emotional Suitcase!

TABLE OF CONTENTS

Bolded key terms found throughout the text have been defined in the glossary.

Foreword

QUESTION: *Why do all of these things keep happening to me?!*

ANSWER: *Because you are strong enough to bounce back. You will be the light and inspiration for generations to come.*

When I sat down to write this book I felt disconnected from the experiences that used to cause me so much pain. I felt disconnected from my history of emotionally traumatic experiences. It seemed like a lifetime ago that teachers were trying to have their way with me. I felt like I had to concentrate to remember the damage that was done when I was molested at 14 years old and hurtful things said by friends and family. I had to ask myself why I felt so disconnected. Was it because I have healed from my past?

I closed my eyes and asked to be reconnected with these experiences and all of the emotions that came with them. Some may say, "Be careful what you ask for." But I knew exactly what I was asking for and I meant it with every ounce of my being.

The only way for me to write this book in a way that would be most effective would be for me to write the words that I needed to hear when I was going through my lowest points. This book must contain the words I needed to hear when I was looking in the mirror crying because I was beginning to hate the person I had become. When I was on my downward spiral with no idea how to get off, I was looking for a sign. I was looking for an answer. This book must contain exactly what I needed to hear at that moment in time so that others may be set free.

If you are on that downward spiral of your emotional rollercoaster, this book is to help you take control. If you have not reached that point in your life then I hope this book helps to prevent you from ever experiencing such pain.

Enjoy. Use it to better yourself. And pay it forward!

Introduction

I want to start by thanking you and congratulating you on your interest in Unpacking the Emotional Suitcase! Your interest may be in unpacking your own emotional suitcase. You may have picked it up to help someone else with their emotional development journey or maybe you just picked it up out of curiosity. Either way the tools and strategies you will learn in this activity guide will help you achieve your goals personally, interpersonally, and professionally.

Two facts about me; I have always been considered the "Emotional One." Secondly, I come from a very proud family and to some, crying is commonly interpreted as a sign of weakness or vulnerability. I can count on one hand the number of times I have seen my mother cry(and she has become the rock/ go-to person in our family.)

I would find myself overly empathetic and crying during commercials, movies, TV shows or even when others would undergo traumatic experiences that had absolutely nothing to do with me. Some would say, "My feelings run deep." With me being such an emotional person it would only make sense that when I experienced my own emotional trauma that the effects could be catastrophic. In efforts to be a stronger role model for my siblings and all of my cousins, I decided I needed to toughen up.

Not knowing the magnitude of the damage I would cause by suppressing my emotional trauma I placed a higher level of importance on upholding my image as a strong and positive woman. I did my best to not care as much about anything. I would relentlessly hold back tears to not look so weak. If I felt myself getting too emotionally involved I would withdraw not appear to be so easily unraveled. I tried to downplay experiences I have gone through in order to not appear so weak.

From the outside looking in I thought I had the world fooled. For a while, I had myself fooled. It wasn't until I was faced with my suppressed experiences that all of those feelings and emotions came rushing back!

For example, at 14 I was molested. I did not tell my parents until I was 23 years old. For all of these years I believed it was my fault, I convinced myself I had brought this on myself so I shouldn't tell anyone because I did not want to get him in trouble. I made myself believe the effects were not that serious because it was not as bad as some of the brutal rapes I read about. I carried on with life not realizing that this experience would rear its ugly head again. When I was 23 years old I found out that a similar situation happened to someone very close to me! When I received the phone call I was furious! I wanted to do something to her predator. Then I stopped and a quiet voice in my head said, "How can you be so protective of her but when you were in a similar situation you did nothing to protect yourself?" I remember standing in my apartment and falling to the floor crying uncontrollably. But the strange thing was as the tears were coming, the images that flashed through my head were images of my own experience from when I was 14. This new experience had some kind of way brought me face to face with my past and I was not ready to face it.

This led me on my emotional development journey to Emotional Success. I hope this process transforms your life like it has transformed mine.

Section A:

Understanding your Emotional Suitcase

Chapter 1

What is the problem?

Imagine this: you and your best friend are sitting together at lunch. You're talking about going to college. You're both very excited about the career options you have chosen and make a plan to stay focused on graduation. As you are leaving the cafeteria someone bumps into you and begins talking trash. What do you do?

a. Keep your goal in mind, dismiss the foolishness and make your way to class.
b. Get in the person's face and begin talking trash back, which may provoke a fight, result in missing class, suspension or arrest.

I am not going to say one is right or wrong. All I want to do is help you make decisions that will help you accomplish your goals.

There are too many individuals losing sight of their goals and failing in life because they continue to get **Emotionally Hijacked.**[1]A person who has been emotionally hijacked has lost control of their own actions. They allow their emotions to take over in a blind rage, causing a great deal of destruction. Often times the response to this type of situation is, "I couldn't help it; I was mad."

No one can fault a person for being mad, embarrassed, scared or experiencing any other emotion. You are entitled to feel how you feel but it's important to remember your emotions do not excuse your actions!

This workbook is designed to help you and those around you to achieve **Emotional Success** and take control of your actions despite how you feel.

READING

Let's begin by addressing one major **misconception**. Just because you are an emotional person does not mean you can't become a master of your own emotions. Everyone deserves emotional stability, happiness and success. Yes, I said it, Emotional success! Everyone always focuses on academic success and financial success yet our society offers very little to support individuals in their journey to emotional success.

Your emotional success is based on your ability to manage your emotions in various situations regardless of the **stimuli**. Please do not confuse controlling your emotions with suppressing them. It is important to acknowledge your emotions. They are real. Maintaining control means to address the situation appropriately and behave in a logical manner that works towards a rational solution.

Not everyone wants to improve emotionally. In order for this to work, it is vital for you to want to be a better person. No matter where you come from, how old you are, no matter your gender, race or cultural background, unpacking your Emotional Suitcase is going to be a journey that requires complete honesty!

Looking yourself in the mirror and facing the truth will at times be the hardest thing to do. However, it's only by being honest with yourself that you can truly develop and identify your steps to emotional success.

ACTIVITY

Think about a time when you recently may have been emotionally hijacked or made a decision that could have jeopardized one of your goals.

Describe the situation:

Which goal did it jeopardize?

LET'S REFLECT!

- It is important to keep your goal in mind. It will prevent you from making mistakes that will ruin your goals.
- Emotional Hijacking is when your emotions have taken over and you have no control over your actions.
- It may not be easy but everyone deserves emotional success.
- The desire to do better and being honest with yourself is going to be two of the most important parts of unpacking your Emotional Suitcase.

Chapter 2

What is an Emotional Suitcase and what's in it?

TRUE STORY:

I had a conversation with a woman who had three children. The oldest of her children was the victim of an unsolved murder. The second oldest seemed to recover just fine from her sister's death. She participated in extracurricular activities and graduated high school with honors. However, on her graduation day, she had a mental break down and was crying hysterically. When her mother took her to see a psychiatrist, the mother was told her daughter was emotionally constipated!

In this true story you see a teenager that experienced emotional trauma, the loss of a loved one. She did not know how to process this experience. Therefore, she suppressed the experience and kept herself busy with school and other activities. Her suitcase became too heavy to carry and she broke down on the day of her graduation. Through this example you see how this habit of suppressing experiences can seem so natural on one hand but on the other hand I hope you see how detrimental it can be to your mental health.

READING

Your **Emotional Suitcase** is a metaphor to describe the place where you store painful, embarrassing, or Emotionally-Traumatic Experiences. These experiences are tucked away because you do not know how to or do not wish to process them. These experiences could range from something as seemingly minor as being embarrassed in elementary school to something as catastrophic as a rape or loss of a loved one.

Because you do not know how or do not wish to process these Emotionally-Traumatic Experiences, you suppress them because you think it is better that way. The truth of the matter is, when you suppress these experiences in your Emotional Suitcase, it is doing you more harm than good. Your suitcase begins to weigh you down as if you were carrying around a bag full of bricks. Have you ever seen people who are always bitter and grumpy? That's because over time their Emotional Suitcase has become so heavy that it stopped them from reaching happiness. This weight can ruin your family, your friendships and stop you from accomplishing your goals. If not handled properly these unprocessed experiences can result in depression, obesity, stress and even death.

The only way to develop and protect yourself from this trend is to break the cycle. This process takes a lot of dedication, honesty and discipline. If you are seriously committed and want to break the cycle, I encourage you to follow the steps I have outlined in this guide. I have used this process personally and have shared with others to help them along their emotional development journey.

The Emotional Processing System

Everyone experiences **Emotionally Traumatic Experiences**. There is not one single person, alive or dead, that has never had an experience that made them sad, angry or embarrassed. The question is, how can two people share an identical experience and one person's world be shattered while the other person bounces back? The difference is in their **Emotional Processing System.** An Emotional Processing System is the system that allows an individual to effectively process Emotionally-Traumatic Experiences properly, storing what needs to be kept and getting rid of what needs to be eliminated.

Remember, in the definition of the Emotional Suitcase, it refers to one's unwillingness or inability to *process* Emotionally-Traumatic Experiences. Most people believe the problem starts with the experience but the problem really starts with a person's inability to effectively process that experience. The best way to break this system down is for me to walk you through it.

Let's compare The Emotional Processing System to a processing system we are all familiar with, the digestive system. Anytime you eat something, the role of your digestive system is to process or sort through what you have eaten. If your digestive system is working properly, it will keep what it needs and eliminate what it does not need. If your digestive system is not working properly, then it will store everything because it does not know how to *process* what you have eaten. You will then become bloated and constipated.

Digestive System

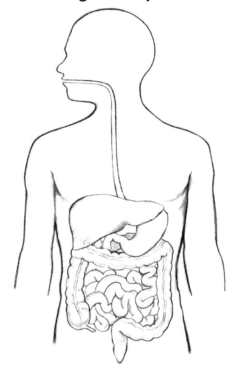

Emotional Processing System

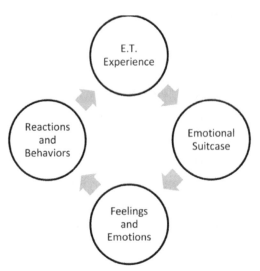

If your digestive system is working properly, it will follow these steps when you eat something:

1. Your digestive system will sort through what you have eaten;
2. It will keep what you need and it will
3. Get rid of what you don't need.

If your digestive system is NOT working properly, most likely it will follow these steps when you eat something:

1. Because your system does not know how to process what you ate, it stores everything.
2. Your belly becomes backed up (bloated and constipated)
3. You begin to see negative reactions like pimples, sickness and disease, letting you know something is wrong!

The same goes for The Emotional Processing System.

If your Emotional Processing System is not working properly, it will follow these steps when you experience emotional trauma:

1. Because your system does not know how to process the Emotionally Traumatic Experience, you store everything (the good, bad and the ugly about the event)
2. Your Emotional Suitcase becomes backed up (emotionally constipated)
3. You begin acting out negatively which is an indication that something is wrong!

ACTIVITY

Unpacking your emotional suitcase is challenging and it will require dedication, honesty and discipline. Make a commitment and stick to it.

Commitment to Myself

I _____(your name) understand that my emotional development journey will not be easy and unpacking my Emotional Suitcase will be extremely challenging but I will DEDICATE myself to seeing it through. I will be HONEST with myself because I understand that is the only way I can improve my flaws. Most importantly, I will have the DISCIPLINE to correct myself and allow myself to be corrected by others if I begin to get off course.

_____   _____

Signature   *Date*

Let's Reflect

- Your **Emotional Suitcase** is a metaphor to describe the place where you store painful, embarrassing or Emotionally-Traumatic Experiences.
- Just because you suppress or hide an experience in your suitcase does not mean it is gone forever. Often times it will come back to haunt you if you do not process it as soon as possible.
- Your Emotional Processing System works just like your digestive system. If you are unable to process what goes in, you will become emotionally constipated.

*I hope that at this point you are curious to find out how to break this cycle. You will find your answers in the next chapter when we cover a process known as **Reverse Engineering.***

Chapter 3

How Do we fix it and where do we start?

TRUE STORY:

I was conducting a workshop with a group of teenage ladies. I walked the young ladies through the reverse engineering cycle. One young lady shared her findings with the group:

Question: **Response:**

Negative Reactions and Behavior: *"Pushing people away before they can get close to me"*

Emotion: *"Fear of being let down or disappointed."*

Experience: *"Father would always say he was coming to get her and never show up."*

In this True Story you read about how this young lady was able

to connect her negative behavior back to an emotion and trace that emotion back to her experience of being let down by her father. For one reason or another, she was unable to process that childhood experience, which led to her feeling the fear of being let down and disappointed and resulted in her pushing people away. It is important to follow these steps outlined in this workbook to get the root of the problem and permanently solve it.

READING

Reverse Engineering is the process of getting to the root of the problem working your way backwards through the Emotional Processing System. I strongly encourage individuals to start breaking the negative Emotional Processing System by first focusing on reactions and behaviors and then working their way backwards. It is best to start with reactions and behaviors because they are much easier to see than feelings, emotions, and even experiences.

Starting with reactions and behaviors, identify the negative or counterproductive behaviors. Trace them back to the emotion(s) you were feeling that prompted these reactions. Once you have identified that emotion(s), you must figure out where the emotion(s) come from. Can you trace it back to an experience? In some cases it may be multiple experiences that have fed this emotion(s). Once you have identified the Emotionally-Traumatic Experience(s) it is time to reprocess these experiences.

At this point, I don't expect you to know all of the answers. All you need is the desire to do better and be better. This workbook provides steps, group and individual activities, true stories and examples to help you along your journey. I strongly encourage you to seek help with this process. Find a counselor, therapist, teacher or a good friend to support you through your journey.

ACTIVITY

Sometimes it is easier to see other people's baggage. Try with a partner or with a character in a movie. Let's start by jotting down some negative or counterproductive behaviors. For each behavior, try to find some corresponding feelings and emotions. If possible, figure out an experience that could have led to these feelings and emotions.

Character Name:_____

Behavior

Feelings

Experience

LET'S REFLECT

- When Reverse Engineering the Emotional Suitcase Cycle, we start with reactions and behaviors because they are the often times the easiest to see.
- We then work our way backwards to trace it back to the root of the problem.

Section B:

Changing Your Behavior

Chapter 4

How do we spot our own reactions and behaviors

TRUE STORY:

I have a cousin who used to behave terribly. She would lie, steal, disrespect and curse out her elders. I tried to talk to her about it but challenging her behavior only made her angrier. One day she told me, "I really want to live a better life and be a better person but I feel like I can't. Every time I try to do better, it's like, stupid people make me upset and I go off again!"

I told her, "It's not going to be easy but you can live a better life and be a better person! You have to set a goal and then take steps. But before you take any steps, think about whether this step is bringing you closer to your goal or taking you further away. If you continue to take more productive steps and less

counterproductive steps, you will find yourself achieving more
and more of your goals."

When trying to spot your counterproductive behaviors try these
three very useful methods: **self-reflection, use your mirrors and
an accountability partner.**

Self Reflection

In order to self-reflect and identify your own counterproductive
behavior, you have to know what you are looking for. For the sake
of your emotional development process, a **counterproductive
behavior** is something that moves you further away from your
goals. Take a moment and think about three major goals you
have. Write them here:

1. _____
2. _____
3. _____

Now it's time to put these goals to use. I must warn you, people
of all ages struggle with this task. Even some of the most
seasoned adults have a hard time identifying their own
counterproductive behaviors.

It is so important to keep your goals in mind. Stick them on your
bathroom mirror so you can see them in the morning when you
brush your teeth! If you are a student and your goal is to
graduate, what decision will you make when someone calls you
out of your name? Will you remember your goal and make the
decision to walk away? Or will you engage in the foolishness,

fight, get suspended or even arrested, miss school and jeopardize graduating on time?

Productive and counterproductive behaviors will not always be so black and white. Sometimes it will be difficult to decide how to categorize them. Just remember, if it moves you closer to your goals, it is productive. If it is moving you further away, it is counterproductive. Nobody is perfect. Sometimes I make counterproductive choices but for the most part I am aware of the difference. When I display counterproductive behavior, I make it my business to get back on track.

Self-reflection is the act of looking at and taking ownership of your own actions. When you stop playing the blame game and take ownership for your actions, you realize you have the power to change your actions to get whatever you want out of life.

USE YOUR MIRRORS

A mirror is traditionally used to see the things you can't see, such as your face, for example. When you get dressed in the morning and you want to make sure your face is clean and your outfit is nice, the mirror is used to either confirm or give you a different point of view.

When it comes to your character, where is the mirror to help you see the things you can't see? People will help you see things you can't see about yourself. Have you ever had someone say, "You are so kind!" or a stranger say, "Why are you so grumpy?" I have learned to use my friends, family and sometimes random strangers as mirrors to see my own personality.

In the **TRUE STORY** I shared at the beginning of this chapter, I was trying to be the mirror for my cousin to help her see her behavior but she was not ready to take ownership of her actions. Once she was ready, I helped her see the things about herself that she could not see. Then she was able to make the necessary adjustments.

WARNING It is important to remember a few things when using people as mirrors:

1. Everyone does not have your best interest at heart and may be out to hurt you;
2. Some people are crazy or simply don't know what they are talking about;
3. Some people are selfish; and
4. There are people out there that do not care.

When using people as mirrors, the goal is to gain a different perspective of both productive and counterproductive behaviors without necessarily taking everyone's opinion as law.

Accountability Partner

Of all of the people that you use as a mirror, the most important person will be your accountability partner. An **accountability partner** is someone who will not allow you to make negative decisions without calling it to your attention. Your accountability partner knows your goals and how important they are to you.

When choosing an accountability partner, make sure:

- this person will tell you the truth, no matter what!
- this person knows the difference between productive and counterproductive behaviors.
- this person supports your goals.
- this person is either an accomplished person or someone on a positive mission.

Identify someone that you want to be your accountability partner. Write them a letter. Here is a sample letter below:

Dear Ms. A,

I have been reading this book titled, Unpacking the Emotional Suitcase and I have decided to set some clear goals and work hard to accomplish them. I know this will not be easy and sometimes I might backslide that is why I am asking you to be my accountability partner and hold me accountable to achieving the goals I have listed below.

Goals:

- *Start my own business*
- *Build a stronger relationship with my parents*
- *Be a nicer person*

Thank you,
Tee

ACTIVITY

Every action that we take either brings us closer or takes us further away from our goals. It is important we learn the difference. Try categorizing these behaviors. Read this person's goal and decide whether their actions and behaviors are taking them closer to or further away from their goals.

For example:

Cameron's goal is to write a book about cartooning and video game design. (Put a check in the appropriate box)

Reaction/Behavior	Closer to Goal	Further Away
Playing games on PS3 all afternoon		
Going to parties		
Reading		
Going to the amusement park		
Fighting		

Your turn! Write down some of your common behaviors in the first column. Decide whether each behavior will bring you closer or take you further away from your goals. *(Put a check in the appropriate box)*

Reaction/Behavior	Closer to Goal	Further Away

ACTIVITY

Use Your Mirrors!

Ask a few people to share a list of your productive and counterproductive behaviors with you. Once you have received the responses, take some time to meditate on what you have learned about yourself from others. Remember not to take every opinion as law. There will be some things that you hear from more than one person. You may want to take a closer look at these opinions.

Step 1:

Find honest and trustworthy friends, colleagues or family members and tell them, *"I have started on an emotional development journey and I need your help. Please be honest and share with me three behaviors I need to improve. Then share three behaviors that are positive and/or productive"*

Step 2:

Meditate on the responses you received. Ask yourself the following questions and fill in the answers below.

1. Did anyone name any negative behaviors that I wasn't aware of? If so, what were they?

   What can I do to change them?

2. Were there any common behaviors? If so, what were they?

LET'S REFLECT

In this chapter, I have shared three major tools to assist you with identifying your counterproductive behaviors.

1. Self Reflection
2. Use your mirrors
3. Find an accountability partner

During this process, you will use different tools for different situations. Sometimes the people around you may not agree with your goals, therefore, they may be unable to give you the best perspective of your negative behaviors. Remember, the opinion of the people you use as mirrors is not to be taken as right or wrong. It is just a different perspective.

Sometimes you may be so distracted that you are not able to self-reflect. It's during those moments you may want to call your accountability partner.

Using the tools and activities shared in this chapter will help you clearly identify your counterproductive behaviors. After identifying them, you have to change them in order to achieve your goals. Now it's time to take it a step further. We have to get to the root of the problem and figure out which emotions we were feeling to cause us to react with each counterproductive behavior.

Chapter 5

How to prevent Emotional Hijacking

TRUE STORY

I recall an incident in middle school where I almost got into a fight. I had never been in a fight before but on this day, that did not matter. It was one of those days things weren't going my way. I was walking down a crowded hallway at school. People kept bumping into me like I didn't even exist. I remember feeling fed up. I couldn't take it anymore. I decided the next person that bumped me was going to get bumped back. The girl that had been picking on me all year was coming down the hall. I threw my shoulder forward and bumped her as hard as I could. She spun around and threatened to slap me. I threw my books to the side, jumped in her face and said, "Slap me!"

My heart was about to jump out of my chest. I could hardly believe what I was doing but I was all in. When she saw that I was not backing down she backed off and said, "You lucky I

don't want to get suspended!"

In this True Story, I identified my negative action as throwing my shoulder forward to nudge someone, then jumping in her face and provoking her to slap me. I was willing to dig deep, so I traced this behavior back to the emotions I was feeling at the time. I felt *fed up*. I also felt *invisible* like people didn't care or my personal space did not matter. As a result of my feelings, I reacted in a way that protected my personal space and let people know I was not invisible.

This situation could have played out very badly. If she had not backed down, we would have started fighting, I might have gotten beat up (since I wasn't a fighter) *AND SUSPENDED! Needless to say, this* was counterproductive to my goal of graduating middle school and it would have been embarrassing! If you think about it, her response was in alignment with her goals. She backed down from the fight because she "didn't want to get suspended."

READING

At times we behave in a way that is unusual or inappropriate because we allow our feelings and emotions to get the best of us. This is called **Emotional Hijacking.** Emotional Hijacking is a situation where a person allows their emotions to take control of their actions. Often times when a person has been Emotionally Hijacked, they do things that they regret and blame it on their emotions. Although, if we take a moment to stop and think before we act, we have a better chance of making more logical decisions that we can be proud of.

It may be difficult for some to identify their emotions. But if we are willing to dig deep enough, we can trace every negative reaction and behavior back to the emotion or set of emotions we were feeling at the time. For example, if you fight often, take a moment to think about what feelings arise just before you get into a fight. Is it anger or embarrassment or does it have something to do with your ego?

Once you have figured out the common emotions you can take it a step further. If you want to prevent yourself from being emotionally hijacked you have to address your feelings before they take over your actions.

If you have a feeling that keeps recurring and causes you to react inappropriately, try finding an alternative reaction. For example, any time I feel _fed up_, I take a moment to myself and sort out the things that are stressing me. I deal with them one at a time. I separate myself from people because I know that I don't interact well when I am fed up. After the negative emotion is handled, I will continue with my day.

Try this ACTIVITY with a partner. Identify some unhealthy reactions and behaviors that person displays. In the chart on the next page, list some possible feelings that person may be feeling to cause this reaction.

In the first column list one more feelings that might lead to a person arguing. In columns 2 and 3 come up with your own reaction or behavior that you have seen in someone else and list three supporting feelings.

Reactions/ Behavior

Possible Feelings

Arguing		
1.	1.	1.
2.	2.	2.
3.	3.	3.

ACTIVITY

Now it's time for a little self reflection! In the previous activity you were practicing on someone else. It is now your turn to dig deep and trace your own actions and behaviors back to the root. In the diagram below write three counterproductive behaviors in the bubbles on the left. Next, take a moment to think of how you feel when you act out the behaviors you have listed. Write the corresponding feeling/emotion in the bubbles on the right.

For example: I FIGHT when I feel THREATENED.

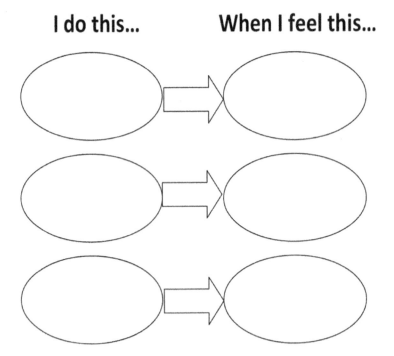

LET'S REFLECT

- Emotional Hijacking is when you allow your emotions to take over and you have no control of your actions.
- Most reactions and behaviors can be traced back to a feeling or emotion.
- The best way to prevent Emotional Hijacking is to have a plan to address your feelings before they take over.

Chapter 6

Don't suppress it... address it!

TRUE STORY

I was working with a group of girls in a Juvenile detention center. We had a discussion about why youth act out and badly behave. One of the young ladies told me she acts out because she noticed that when she properly behaves, she does not get any attention. When we got deeper into the conversation, we traced her illegal behavior and thoughts back to a simple emotion; she felt forgotten. When she feels forgotten, she behaves badly to get attention.

The young lady was so convinced that she had solved her problem of feeling forgotten or overlooked that she could not see how her actions were taking her down a road of destruction. If she could rewind the clock to when she first started feeling this emotion, I would tell her to share this with her accountability partner so they could work together to find a healthier way to address that forgotten feeling without leading her down a path to jail.

My heart goes out to this young lady. She has become so lost by suppressing her feeling and trying to find solutions on her own. But she is not the only one. Other young ladies in the group were saying the same thing. As a matter of fact, if you are reading this book, you may also feel the same way. Let's analyze this method of thinking and see how we can address this feeling before it becomes a bigger problem for us.

READING

Imagine doing all that hard work tracing your reactions and behaviors back to emotions, only to find that the emotions you were feeling were silly or stupid! What do you do? Laugh it off and suppress it? NO! There is no feeling or emotion too big or too small to address!

"I got angry for nothing... that was silly."

"How do I tell someone I feel forgotten? That's dumb!"

Have you ever seen someone explode out of the blue? And when you ask what happened they can't really explain why they reacted the way they did? This used to happen to me all the time! I used to suppress my feelings because I thought they weren't important. Imagine suppressing your feelings is like blowing air into a balloon. If you keep blowing air into this balloon long enough, what will eventually happen? It will pop! If we have certain feelings or emotions that we do not address, they will build up and like the balloon, we will eventually pop or explode!

Talking to your friends sometimes is not always the best idea. They may be experiencing the same problems as you are. For example, if a young lady feels insecure because of the way she looks and tries to get advice from her friend, who is also insecure, it may not be the best advice to help her process the negative feelings she is having. **This reminds me of an old saying I used to hear growing up, "It's like the blind leading the blind!"**

This is where having a wise and clear thinking accountability partner will really come in handy. Remember, if your accountability partner ever makes you feel like any of your feelings are not important, I would encourage you to find a new accountability partner.

ACTIVITY

Take a moment and think of a time when you tried to suppress a feeling you had because you thought it was not a big deal. Think about it further and ask yourself these questions:

- Was it a good idea or a bad idea to suppress this feeling?
- If you had to do it all over again would you make a different decision? Why or why not?

Now share this situation with a partner and ask your partner what they would have done and why.

- There is no feeling or emotion too large or too small to address.
- Suppressing feelings can be bad for your emotional and mental health.
- Be sure to take advice from wise, clear thinking individuals.
- Your accountability partner should never make you feel like your feelings are not important.

Section C:

Reprocessing Emotionally-Traumatic Experiences

Chapter 7

Unpacking the Emotional Suitcase

TRUE STORY:

I was helping a young lady unpack her Emotional Suitcase. I started by acknowledging her rapidly-declining behavior. I asked her what was going on. I explained the Emotional Suitcase process to her. She turned to me and said, "I got a lot of stuff in my suitcase."

I started sharing ways she could unpack her suitcase. She told me she doesn't like to talk and wanted to know if she could write it out. "Of course!" I said.

After she wrote out her story, she asked if I could help her turn it into a poem. I showed her the method I use to write most of my poetry. She wrote one of the most beautiful poetry pieces I've ever read! Even though she did not feel comfortable talking to me about what she had in her Emotional Suitcase, she was able to use poetry to tell me that losing her father and being abandoned by her mother has made her really sad and that is why she has been misbehaving.

READING

Unpacking Your Emotional Suitcase is when you express your Emotionally-Traumatic Experiences through various forms, including (but not limited to):

- Poetry
- Lyrics
- Journal
- Blogs
- Movie scripts
- Books
- Short stories
- Talking
- Singing (original lyrics)

Unpacking Your Emotional Suitcase equals expression which is healthy for you. The opposite of expression is suppression. Suppression is the act of resisting feelings and emotions as they arise. Suppressing your feelings and emotions leads to an overweight Emotional Suitcase.

If your suitcase is already heavy, it's not too late. In order to unpack it, you must learn the art of expression. Figure out which form of expression works best with your personality and begin expressing those emotions, feelings and experiences. You will find yourself unloading your suitcase piece by piece. Over time, your emotional load will become lighter. When a person gets in the habit of choosing expression over suppression, it becomes much easier to maintain a healthy balance in your Emotional Suitcase.

It is through telling your story that you will be able to trace your feelings and emotions back to the experiences that produced them. In the beginning, I strongly encourage you to limit the number of people you share your story with. If you are embarrassed, ashamed or simply have not processed your experiences, then nine times out of ten, your story is unprocessed and still owns you. When your story owns you, people can use it against you to embarrass you, make you feel inferior or even to provoke you.

When you own your story, you can use it to inspire others. You fully understand that your past does not define who you are today nor does it determine where you are going. If you own your story and someone tries to use it against you, it will be more difficult for it to faze you because you have reached a certain level of peace with your past.

If you want to learn how to own your story here are a few tips:

#1. Practice expressing your feelings, emotions and experiences with select individuals until you feel comfortable to share it with others.

#2. Reprocess your Emotionally-Traumatic Experiences using the tools shared in chapter 9.

#3. Turn your pain into power like the examples shared in chapter 12.

ACTIVITY

Let test it out:

Step 1: Select a form of expression that best suits your personality type.

Step 2: Think of a situation that happed recently that was embarrassing, made you sad or made you upset.

Step 3: Using your form of expression, share your experience.

For example: If you chose poetry, write a poem.

If you chose blog, write a blog post.

(If you need more space, use an extra sheet of paper.)

_____

_____

_____

_____

_____

_____

_____

_____

_____

LET'S REFLECT

- There are unlimited ways to express yourself.
- Expression is the opposite of suppression.
- It's never too late to start unpacking your Emotional Suitcase.

Chapter 8

How to know if your EMOTIONALLY-TRAUMATIC EXPERIENCE has been processed

TRUE STORY

When I was 14 years old, I was molested. I didn't tell anyone, with the exception of a few of my closest friends. I had written some poetry about it and assumed it did not affect me. When I was 22, I found out that a similar situation happened to someone very close to me. I was furious when I received the phone call and wanted to cause harm to her predator. Then I stopped and a quiet voice in my head said, "How can you be so protective of her but when you were in a similar situation you did nothing to protect yourself?" I remember standing in my apartment and falling to the floor crying uncontrollably. The strange thing was that as the tears were coming, the images that flashed through my head were images of my own experience from when I was 14. In some kind of way, this new experience had brought me face to face with my past. I became emotionally hijacked and I was not ready to face it.

This True Story shows that even though you may think your Emotionally-Traumatic Experience has been processed, it may be something that will bring you face to face with it again and you will learn you have more work to do.

After completing the *Unpacking the Emotional Suitcase* program, I was able to reprocess that experience. Now I can hold a conversation about this topic without coming to tears.

READING

We have been speaking a lot about processed and unprocessed experiences. It is important to know that an unprocessed experience is an experience that has been stored along with the heavy feelings such as grudge, blame, guilt, regret, embarrassment, etc.

I was giving a presentation about unpacking the Emotional Suitcase to a group of educators when one lady raised her hand and asked, "How do you know if the experience is processed or not?" The answer I gave her is the same guidance I will share with you.

Unfortunately, there is not a set procedure or thermometer to test whether or not your experiences have been processed. The best thing to do is reflect on the experience and try to talk or write about it. Observe the feelings that come up when you talk

64

about that issue. Here are some questions to ask yourself:

- **What emotions originally stemmed from the Emotionally-Traumatic Experience?**

    It's important to take yourself back to the experience and think about what emotions you felt during the experience and immediately afterwards. This information is good to know and will help you with some of the other questions and the rest of your emotional development journey

- **What emotions do I feel about the experience now?**

    The answer to this question may or may not be different from the previous question but it may be equally as important. For example, if a wife has experienced domestic violence from her husband, she may have felt inferior, unworthy, etc. Let's say she gets out of that situation. As time passes, she may begin to feel bitter and pessimistic towards marriage and men. It is important to monitor the progression of your emotions and experiences when you suppress feelings. In some cases individuals will become calloused and begin taking out deep rooted frustrations on innocent people.

- **Have I allowed myself enough time to feel the emotions?**

    Sometimes individuals will tell themselves to, "stop being so emotional" or "get over it!" It is important to allow yourself the time to feel and acknowledge the emotions associated with your experience. I am not saying burst into tears on stage from an embarrassing trip or fall but get to a safe place before you begin unpacking your suitcase. As you acknowledge the emotions that came from that experience, process them with the steps outlined in the next section. (*meditation can be very helpful with this one*)

- **Did I ever try to not feel the emotions?**

    Have you ever told yourself you were silly or stupid for feeling a certain way? For example, maybe after a breakup or the loss of a pet? It's important not to rush through the grieving period. Every Emotionally-Traumatic Experience has a grieving period. Some may be shorter than others. Nonetheless, this is the time to feel and acknowledge the feelings that stem from the Emotionally-Traumatic Experience. During this time, there is a delicate balancing act that must be mastered. Although it is important not to cut your grieving period short, one cannot grieve forever. Work on processing your experiences and then focusing on solutions.

- **Did I ever try to not think about the experience?**

    Some people may believe if they don't think about it, the entire experience will just go away. Well, it's not true. Attempting to think it away or not think about it is the same thing as suppression. More often than not, these situations backfire. These experiences will usually pile up and one small incident will be the straw that breaks the camel's back, meaning there was too much weight stacked up you were attempting to ignore and one small thing that caused you to break down. If you process your experiences as you experience them, you will not have so much to clean up later on.

- **If someone wanted to talk to me about the experience today, would I be okay?**

    This question is to determine whether or not you are prepared to come face to face with the experience without crumbling or becoming Emotionally Hijacked. This question can be tricky. A person may have processed an experience but makes a conscious decision not to talk about due to various circumstances. However, if you are not talking about it because it evokes certain painful or embarrassing emotions, then you may have more work to do.

- **Could I give advice to someone else on how to overcome a similar experience?**

  One of the best ways to give advice to a person is if you have overcome a similar experience. Try it for yourself. Write a letter to someone (real or fake) telling them your story of how you overcame emotional trauma and then advise them on how they can overcome trauma, too. If you are unable to advise, it is possible that you may still be in need of advice.

ACTIVITY

Think of a real experience that was emotionally-traumatic, big or small. Pretend you have met someone who has just gone through the same experience as you. Write them a letter to advise them how to overcome that experience. Be sure to tell them about your experience, including how you felt, the things you did to overcome and how you are feeling now.

_____

_____

_____

_____

_____

_____

_____

_____

_____

_____

_____

_____

_____

_____

LET'S REFLECT

- An unprocessed experience is an experience that has been stored along with the heavy feelings such as grudge, blame, guilt, regret, embarrassment, etc.
- If your story owns you and hijacks you emotionally, then your experience still needs to be processed.
- When it comes to processed vs. unprocessed, one of the most significant indications is whether a person can face the experience and own that story.

Chapter 9

Reprocessing EMOTIONALLY-TRAUMATIC EXPERIENCES

TRUE STORY

Imagine growing up believing that your mother hated you. It was as if you could get nothing right! She fussed and cursed at you. You cried and swore that as soon as you turned 18 you would get as far away from her as you could. You finally turn 18. On your high school graduation day, your mother turns to you with tears in her eyes and tells you, "I am so proud of you! I know I have been pretty hard on you but it was all I knew. I had no real supervision growing up and that's why I was a teen mother that didn't finish high school. I promised myself that I would never let you be a failure like me. And that's why I was so hard on you."

Would this change things? Could you find it in your heart to forgive your mother? Could you put all of that anger and pain aside now that you have a different perspective?

When it comes to reprocessing experiences, the goal is to adjust your perspective about the event. Everyone experiences emotional trauma but the difference between a healthy person and an unhealthy person depends on your perspective of these Emotionally-Traumatic Experiences.

For example, if two people experienced the same form of abuse, the unhealthy person is the one that carries around the embarrassment, guilt, shame, fear, and blame. It's possible they believe it was their fault in some way. The healthy person has a lighter perspective because that person probably understands that the abuse occurred because of the ill intentions of the abuser, not the victim. The unhealthy person will be scared and struggle to form healthy relationships while the healthy person will use this same experience to be wise and precautious when making decisions about future relationships.

Some experiences may be easier to reprocess than others. But it's okay! This is an emotional development *journey*. For some of your Emotionally-Traumatic Experiences, you will find it easy to redirect your beliefs about the event. However, others may find it much more difficult. Imagine you are digging up two trees from your back yard. The first tree was planted about one year ago, so the roots have not grown too deep and it's easier for you to uproot this tree. The second tree is over 20 years old. This will take a lot more time and difficulty because the roots of this tree run deep! Just like your experiences. The suppressed childhood memories that are lying in your Emotional Suitcase will likely be more difficult to reprocess than something that occurred within the past six months to a year.

Tips on processing experiences

Here are some strategies I have seen work:

- **Find the silver lining**
  Amidst chaos, an optimistic person will often find something positive about the situation. This is called "finding the silver lining." Sometimes the situation can be so dark and painful that it seems impossible to find one but remaining optimistic will help you overcome and reprocess Emotionally-Traumatic Experiences.

  For example: A woman who is trying to process the death of a loved one looks at the situation optimistically and is grateful that her loved one no longer has to experience the pain and suffering he/she went through in their final days.

- **Stop playing the blame game and focus on solutions**
  People sometimes spend all of their energy and attention looking for someone to blame for the situation. I have found if we focus more attention on finding a solution to the problem or a plan for how to overcome it, then we can bounce back quicker and have a healthier recovery.

  Like they say, *"Don't cry over spilled milk."*

- **Take ownership of your actions**
  Sometimes our actions land us in situations that leave us vulnerable for emotional trauma. After you experience an Emotionally-Traumatic Experience, take a moment to

reflect over the entire experience and see if there was anything you could have done differently. Take note of these actions so that you can avoid repeating them and leaving yourself vulnerable in the future. I find that when I use this strategy it makes me feel more powerful and less like a victim.

- **The past is the past; let it stay there** *(if you are currently in the situation, GET OUT!)*
  Your past does not have to dictate your future. Just because you have had Emotionally-Traumatic Experiences happen in the past does not mean you have to carry the weight of those experiences into your future.

  For example: If you were physically abused by a man in the past this does not mean that all men will abuse you. You do not have to treat every man like he is abusive. It's okay to allow yourself to be vulnerable to those who deserve it. Watch out for the signs and give yourself a chance to heal.

  If you are currently in a situation where you are experiencing emotional trauma, be sure to EXPLICITYLY let the other parties involved know that you are uncomfortable with the situation. If it continues, seek the appropriate assistance in getting out of that situation. It is NEVER okay to be abused!

- **Change your perspective**
  A lot of people find their healing in changing their perspective on their experience. There are many ways to go about this. One way is to put yourself in someone else's shoes. If the experience involves another party, putting yourself in their shoes will help you see the event from their eyes. Sometimes this is helpful, other times it is not.

Another way to put yourself in someone else's shoes is to imagine someone less fortunate than you. This can help you to be appreciative of the things you have.

You can also change your perspective by talking to an unbiased person. Sometimes people will agree with you to make you feel good but an unbiased person will help you see your story from another perspective you might find it easier to process.

ACTIVITY

Mariah is crying. You asked her why. She told you that her parents have been fighting and they are getting a divorce. Her father will be moving out next week and she feels like it is all her fault. She is really sad and does not want her parents to split up.

Mariah has decided to confide in you. Now choose one or more of the strategies from the reprocessing chapter to help Mariah reprocess this Emotionally-Traumatic Experience. In the space below, right what you would say to Mariah then right the strategies that you used.

_____

_____

_____

_____

_____

_____

_____

_____

_____

_____

_____

LET'S REFLECT

- Changing perspectives can often help in reprocessing experiences.
- Experiences are like trees. The ones that are newer are easier to dig up but the ones that were planted long ago may require more effort and maybe a little assistance.
- There are many different ways to reprocess Emotionally Traumatic Experiences.

Section D:

Strategies to Help You on your Journey

Chapter 10

Incentivize Your Journey

TRUE STORY

There was a young lady who was a close friend of my family. She had anger management issues. She had tried counseling but she could never stay committed to it. For years, she offended family and strangers with no remorse. When she became pregnant, one of her biggest fears was that her baby would be mean and rude. She decided she would attend some anger management classes to help her resolve her issues. This time, she stayed committed and has been able to better manager her anger.

She had set a goal to resolve her anger management issues before becoming pregnant, however, she was unable to stay committed because she had no incentive. In this chapter, you will learn more about the difference between goals and incentives and how to use them to help you stay on track.

Incentivize your journey

Unpacking your Emotional Suitcase is going to be challenging. One of the best ways to avoid giving up is to make a list of goals. For each goal, write three to four reasons why it is important to achieve that goal. We will call these reasons **incentives.**

An incentive is a reward offered to increase productivity. These incentives will come in handy when you feel like giving in or doing something to jeopardize accomplishing your goals. It is not enough to just have a goal, the true value rests in why your goal is important to you. In the example given below, the goal is to get a job. The value does not rest in having a job. The true value rests in what having a job can do for you.

When coming up with your incentives, try including people that look up to you, like your children, siblings, cousins, mentees, etc. Be honest. There may be an incentive that appears shallow or selfish to others but use it if it works for you! *(Example: I want to be a famous singer so I can hear everyone screaming my name)* Imagining a crowd chanting your name could be the motivation you need in times of weakness. Whatever your incentives are, be honest with yourself and make your list.

For example: My goal is to: Get a job

a) *I want to get a job so I can have money to buy the things I want and need.*
b) *I want to get a job so I do not have to depend on other people.*
c) *I want to get a job so I can prove to my family that I am growing up.*

ACTIVITY

Now it's your turn:

Goal #1: _____

    a) _____

    b) _____

    c) _____

Goal #2:_____

    a) _____

    b) _____

    c) _____

Goal #3:_____

    a) _____

    b) _____

    c) _____

Now, write your incentives on sticky notes and post them around your room, office or bathroom to remind you to stay focused.

Obstacles

What are some obstacles that have stopped or slowed you down in the past from seeing progress? This question is very important. If we can recognize those things that have stopped us in the past, then we can create a game plan to overcome obstacles if they ever come up in the future. So, take a moment and reflect. Then write a list of any obstacles that have ever come between you and your goals. No obstacle is too big or small.

Obstacles:

_____

_____

_____

_____

_____

_____

_____

_____

_____

Chapter 11

Customize your plan

TRUE STORY:

When I was younger I had a friend that like to skip school. Before we became friends, I had skipped class before but I was too afraid to actually leave the school building. She said, "C'mon it will be fine. I do it all the time!"

One year, on her birthday, she decided we were going to skip school. On the same day, her mother planned to surprise her with balloons and birthday cake. When she found out she was not at school she started looking for her and found us at the McDonalds around the corner from our apartments. Her mom called my mom and told her everything! We got in so much trouble that day!

READING

I had a goal to graduate but I did not do a great job of keeping that goal in mind. I knew my friend liked to skip school, which was not in alignment with my goal. I knew that one of my weaknesses was peer pressure. I allowed myself to be pressured into doing something that got me in trouble and jeopardized my goals.

Most of the time, if we are honest with ourselves, we already know what our weaknesses are. We must put systems in place so we can stop temptation before it even starts. If I want to stop doing drugs and I know that Sarah and Joe like to peer-pressure me, then it would be in my best interest to not hang with those individuals. List some weaknesses and negative influences that have slowed you down or stopped you from accomplishing your goals in the past:

Negative Influences	Weaknesses
Example: Sarah	*Example: Spending money on shoes*

Note- I know naming negative influences might be a little difficult because they might be a family member, your best friend or even your significant other! It's okay. Remember this journey is all about honesty. Be honest with yourself about your negative influences. You can still love them; you might just have to love them from a distance.

ACTIVITY

Motto/Creed

Combine your weaknesses and your incentives to create a personal motto or creed. Revisit this when you wake up, before you go to bed or when you feel tempted to backslide.

Example: *It is my goal to get a job this year so I can afford the things I want and need without depending on anyone else. I know that sometimes when I hang out with Sarah, I am tempted to smoke. I know that will stand in the way of getting and keeping a job so I will spend less time with her and more time with Crystal. I deserve this job and I will stop at nothing to make this goal a reality!*

Your turn:

_____

_____

_____

_____

_____

_____

Chapter 12

Empower others

TRUE STORY

There is a boy named Jalen who has Tourette's syndrome, which is a condition that causes your body to make repeated and uncontrolled jerking movements and sounds. Students at school would pick on him because of his condition, which was embarrassing for Jalen. He decided to take ownership of his situation. He started his own company and began speaking about his condition. He created wristbands that he sells to raise money to find a cure and to raise awareness. He was able to get some big attention and had celebrities and movie stars wearing his wristbands too! This is a perfect example of someone who turned their pain into power!

READING

"One of the most rewarding ways to heal yourself is to help someone else." -Tierica Berry

TURN YOUR PAIN INTO POWER:

OWN YOUR STORY

Earlier you read about owning your story as opposed to your story owning you. It is impossible to turn your pain into power if your story still owns you.

If your story owns you then I can use your story to make you cry, provoke you, or to embarrass you. This goes back to Emotional Hijacking and the inability to control the reactions. I am not saying that you will never cry or feel sad or angry about the experience you have had. The difference is, when you own your story you are able to manage your emotions better. You can tell your story without completely falling apart.

If you have not owned your story yet, it's okay! Remember this is a development *journey*. Most of the time this process does not happen overnight.

TELL YOUR STORY

Get in the habit of telling your story. People love a good story! Think about it: some of the best songs, movies and television shows are just telling a great story. As you tell your story, you may find confidence and power in sharing with others.

Sometimes you may feel like, "I am the only person in the world that has experienced this..." But I am here to tell you, there is someone out there that has experienced it too. Most of the issues and experiences we face in life are more common than we think. There is comfort in knowing you are not alone. There is even more comfort in helping someone else survive what you have survived and processed. But only when you are ready.

ACTIVITY

Identify one of your personal Emotionally Traumatic Experiences. Think about how you can share your story to help others who might be struggling with the same Emotionally Traumatic Experience. Can you share your story through a song? Maybe you can write a book, a poem, or maybe give a speech. The choice is yours. Be sure to incorporate the following things in your story:

- What is your Emotionally Traumatic Experience?
- Feelings and emotions came from this experience
- Any challenges you had processing the experience (if any)
- How you survived and processed your experience

Ask your accountability partner when is the best time for you to open up and share your story with others. Also talk to your accountability partner about how to share your story with individuals that can relate.

LET'S REFLECT

- Owning your story will help you from becoming Emotionally Hijacked.
- If your story still owns you, it's okay! These things take time.
- You can help speed up your recovery time by sharing your stories of triumph and victories with others.

Resources

Glossary

Accountability Partner- a wise and clear thinking individual that will hold you accountable to the goals you have set and let you know when you are straying from your path.
Example: Teacher, parent, counselor, mentor, coach, etc.

Counterproductive Behavior- is any behavior that stops or slows you down from accomplishing your goals. Often times these are negative behaviors.
Example: Fighting, promiscuity, drugs, self inflicted pain, etc.

Emotional Constipation- the conflict that occurs when an individual is unable to process Emotionally Traumatic Experiences and their Emotional Processing System becomes backed up.

Emotional Success- one's ability to manage their actions in various situations regardless of the stimuli.

Emotional Suitcase- is a metaphor used to describe the place individuals store painful, embarrassing, and traumatic experiences because they do not know how or do not wish to process them.

Emotional Processing System- the system that allows an individual to effectively process Emotionally-Traumatic Experiences properly, storing what needs to be kept and getting rid of what needs to be eliminated.

Emotionally-Traumatic Experience- any distressing event that causes an overwhelming amount of stress and is challenging for one to cope with the feelings and emotions related to that experience.
Example: Loss of a loved one, rape, war, domestic violence, etc.

Incentives- a list of reasons why you want to accomplish your goals that will incite action or greater effort. A reward.

Processed Experience- an emotionally traumatic experience that an individual has given themselves the appropriate time to grieve and come to peace with the experience.

Productive Behavior- any behavior that gets you closer to your goals. These are often positive behaviors.
Examples: studying, working, starting a business, etc.

Reverse Engineering- is the process of getting to the root of the problem working your way backwards through the Emotional Processing System.

Suppression- the act of resisting feelings and emotions as they arise.

Unpacking the Emotional Suitcase- an emotional development process in which individuals reprocess their emotionally traumatic experiences to lighten their load and achieve emotional success.

Unprocessed Experience- an emotionally traumatic experience that has been stored along with the heavy weight of grudge, blame, guilt, regret, embarrassment, etc.

Common Questions

and Concerns

1. **Do I have to be vulnerable?**

    This is common concern for a lot of individuals, young and old. Often we are taught we have to be so tough or so perfect. We are made to believe that crying is a sign of weakness.

    This is the very reason why so many people that need help will never get it. There are people who have lived their entire lives unhappy because they were too afraid to open up and get the help they needed.

    I do not encourage you to share your vulnerability with anyone and everyone. Remember, there are people that set out to hurt you or bring you down.

    Save your vulnerability for someone whom you have built a relationship with, someone who has agreed to help you, such as a counselor, family member, mentor or a friend.

    After you have decided on whom to open up to, then the two of you can come up with solutions to overcome some of your most crippling emotions!

2. **If the feeling is too small should I just let it go?**

    Absolutely not! There is no negative feeling or emotion too small to be addressed. Along my emotional development journey, I found that most of my big issues came from a lot of smaller issues that were not resolved because I thought they were too insignificant to call to anyone's attention.

    If you have an emotion that you think is too small, still share it with someone you can trust and come up with a strategy plan to overcome it. You might be surprised at how confident you will become after overcoming several small victories.

3. **If the emotion is too big, who can I tell?**

    Sometimes the emotions you are feeling can be overwhelming, i.e. the emotions that come from rape, physical abuse, etc. Sometimes it may feel like if you share this experience with someone, you may be burdening them with your sorrows. You may believe that it is so overwhelming that no one can help you. But I promise you, there is someone that you can talk to about these emotions. Just be sure that the person you find is experienced and prepared to give you some useful advice.

4. **Are all feelings attached to something?**

    Yes. Our character, opinions and views of the world are all based on our experiences. For example, the way we feel about rainy days may depend on what rainy days represented in our childhood.

ALSO AVAILABLE:

www.AffirmativeExpression.com

ABOUT THE AUTHOR

Tierica Berry is an emotional success strategist and women's empowerment leader and dedicates most of her time to delivering staff development training and youth presentations. With heavy emphasis on emotional success Tierica has managed to motivate and redirect some of the most troubled youth with her engaging and relevant programs. In partnership with Hustle University and the Make a Way Program her organization services various types of youth organizations from public school districts to youth detention centers. Tierica has received national recognition for her creative writing program, The Anthology Project, and she continues to make sustainable impact with her latest initiatives Unpacking the Emotional Suitcase, and A Woman's Standard. As a published author of multiple empowerment books Tierica is determined to leave a lasting legacy as she continues to express herself affirmatively!

To learn more about the relevant programs and impactful initiatives please visit:
www.AffirmativeExpression.com

For booking information please email your request to:
Info@AffirmativeExpression.com

Made in the USA
Columbia, SC
26 June 2021